CONTENTS

NATURAL DISASTERS

TORNADOES

Luke Thompson

Children's Press
A Division of Grolier Publishing
New York / London / Hong Kong / Sydney
Danbury, Connecticut

Book Design: MaryJane Wojciechowski
Contributing Editors: Jennifer Ceaser and Rob Kirkpatrick

Photo Credits: Cover, pp. 13, 19 © Faidley/Agliolo/International Stock; pp. 4, 5, 11, 29, 38 © Artville Stock Images; pp. 7, 25 © Bettmann/Corbis; pp. 8, 9 © Kevin R. Morris/Corbis; pp. 15, 35 © Warren Faidley/International Stock; p. 21 © Lambert/Archive Photos; pp. 22, 23, 31, 33, 34 © Associated Press/AP Wide World Photos; p. 27 © Associated Press/University of Chicago; p. 37 © NOAA

Visit Children's Press on the Internet at:
http://publishing.grolier.com

Cataloging-in-Publication Data

Thompson, Luke.
    Tornadoes / by Luke Thompson.
      p. cm. – (Natural disasters)
    Includes bibliographical references and index.
    Summary: This book explains how tornadoes form, describes
 the technology used in predicting tornadoes, and offers safety
 tips for surviving this natural disaster.
    ISBN 0-516-23371-8 (lib. bdg.) – ISBN 0-516-23571-0 (pbk.)
    1. Tornadoes—Juvenile literature. [1. Tornadoes] I. Title. II. Series.
    QC955.2.T48 2000   00-029524
    551.55'3—dc21

On the morning of March 25, 1925, a typical thunderstorm began forming over the western United States. It rolled across the Great Plains of Kansas and grew stronger. Somewhere above the open fields of Missouri, at 1:01 P.M., the storm went from bad to worse. The winds inside the storm began to move in circles. The clouds moved in circles, too. The winds eventually formed a swirling, cone-shaped mass, called a funnel. The winds inside the funnel were moving faster than 100 miles (16 km) per hour. The funnel touched down on the ground. The Tri-State Tornado had begun.

Most tornadoes that strike the United States last from fifteen minutes to an hour. The Tri-State Tornado lasted more than three hours. Most tornadoes travel at speeds of 15 to 25 miles (24 to 40 km)

This cone-shaped mass of swirling wind is called a funnel.

per hour. This tornado traveled at a speed of 60 miles (96 km) per hour. The Tri-State Tornado lasted for so long and traveled so fast, it made a trail 220 miles (354 km) long across three different states—Missouri, Illinois, and Indiana.

When the Tri-State Tornado finally ended, 689 people were dead, more than 2,000 were injured, and millions of dollars' worth of property had been destroyed. It was the worst tornado in the history of the United States.

The winds that swirl inside a tornado are the fastest and strongest winds on Earth. Tornadoes have been known to pick up houses and throw them hundreds of feet. Tornadoes have driven bits of straw through solid pieces of wood. They have picked up cows, carried them hundreds of yards in the air, and put the animals back on the ground without hurting them. There are thousands of

The 1925 Tri-State Tornado destroyed millions of dollars' worth of property.

tornado tales. Some are just weird stories; others are accounts of extreme violence. As do other natural disasters, tornadoes have the potential to kill a lot of people and do a lot of damage.

In the United States, about one thousand tornadoes strike each year. Annually, these storms kill approximately forty-two people. In the first three months of 2000, twenty-nine tornadoes hit the United States, resulting in eighteen deaths. Since 1998, about 2,700 tornadoes have caused the deaths of more than two hundred Americans. The homes and other property destroyed by these monster storms reaches into the billions of dollars.

CHAPTER ONE

A MONSTER IN THE CLOUDS

On April 4, 1977, a powerful tornado tore through the city of Birmingham, Alabama. The wind speeds of this tornado are believed to have reached 300 miles (483 km) per hour.

Birmingham resident Georgia Mayal and her family were very lucky to have survived the tornado. The Mayals were on their front porch watching as the dark, threatening storm gathered speed and moved toward them. They ran inside and crowded into a small closet. Then the tornado struck the Mayal house.

"The whole house exploded. It was like a bomb going off," Georgia recalled. The closet floor collapsed, and Georgia and her family fell into the basement. They landed safely on top of the clothes that were in the closet. But the house, which had just crumbled beneath their feet, was falling on top of them. Amazingly, the Mayals were not badly hurt.

Houses are no match for a tornado's destructive winds.

TORNADOES

When the Mayals were sure the tornado was done, they crawled to safety through a hole.

Georgia and her family survived one of the worst tornadoes in history. The Mayals may have lost their house in the storm, but twenty-two of their neighbors lost their lives. Hundreds of people in Birmingham were left homeless.

WHAT IS A TORNADO?

A tornado is a spinning column of air that comes into contact with Earth's surface. Normally, you would not be able to see air, but tornadoes gather clouds and dust as they move. With all of these particles swirling around, the tornado becomes darker and its shape becomes very clear. The whirling dust and clouds form a funnel. Inside the funnel, winds are moving at speeds of 40 to 318 miles (64 to 512 km) per hour. These winds create a vacuum, which works just like a vacuum

Tornadoes are visible because they gather clouds and dust as they move.

cleaner, sucking up everything in its path. However, tornado funnels can move enormous objects, such as houses, bridges, and cars.

HOW DOES A TORNADO FORM?

Tornadoes are produced by severe thunderstorms. Thunderstorms are very common, but only a small fraction of them will become tornadoes. Of the 16 million thunderstorms that strike our planet every year (that's 45,000 a day), fewer than 2,000 will result in tornadoes.

For a tornado to occur, the thunderstorm has to have the exact balance of temperature, humidity (moisture), and wind. A tornadic thunderstorm is a storm that is capable of producing a tornado. A tornadic thunderstorm is created when warm, moist air is trapped under a layer of cold, dry air and another layer of warm, dry air. If weather conditions are right, the two top layers become unstable. The bottommost layer of warm, moist air is then able to push through the layers above it.

The moist air is propelled upward by winds near Earth's surface. These winds also cause the air to rotate. The wind spirals quickly

A tornado is produced by a tornadic thunderstorm.

upward—at speeds of up to 150 miles (241.5 km) per hour. The moist, swirling wind that blows up from Earth's surface is called an updraft. The updraft is what fuels a thunderstorm and keeps it going. The stronger the updraft, the stronger the thunderstorm, and the more likely a tornado is to form.

As the air rises higher into the atmosphere, it begins to condense. When air condenses, it changes from a vapor (water in the form of a gas) into a liquid (rain). The process of condensation produces a lot of rain, lightning, and heat. This heat is the main source of energy in a tornadic thunderstorm.

WHEN AND WHERE TORNADOES STRIKE

Tornadoes seem capable of popping up (or down) almost anywhere. These powerful storms are reported every year in Australia, Brazil, Canada, Great Britain, India, Italy, Japan, and South Africa. Yet certain areas have more tornadoes than others. This is because tornadoes are controlled by the weather. Because Earth's weather is based on patterns, Earth's tornadoes are, too. The United States happens to have a weather pattern that spawns more tornadoes than does the weather pattern in any other country.

March through July is the peak time for tornado season in the United States. During those months, an average of five tornadoes touch

Most tornadoes strike late in the day.

down each day. Most tornadoes occur in the afternoon and evening. Tornadoes happen more often during certain months and times of the day because of weather conditions. These conditions are based on a combination of heat, wind speed, and air pressure. Wherever there is warm, moist air; low air pressure; and shifting winds; there is a good chance that severe thunderstorms will form. These conditions usually are present in the spring months and late in the day, when there is more hot air in the atmosphere. Some of these thunderstorms will be severe enough to produce tornadoes.

Tornado Alley

Most tornadoes occur in the central United States in an area called Tornado Alley. Tornado Alley stretches across several states, including Iowa, Kansas, Oklahoma, Missouri, Nebraska, and Texas. Tornado Alley has been the setting for some of the most disastrous storms of the past century.

All of the elements needed to form tornadoes—warm and cold air, strong winds, moisture, and shifting winds—can be found in Tornado Alley. In spring, a weather pattern called the jet stream moves from the west and settles over the central United States. The jet stream brings with it strong winds and low air pressure. The low air pressure draws in moist air from the Gulf of Mexico. The combination of hot air, cold air, and shifting winds produces severe thunderstorms. Because so many thunderstorms occur in this area, there is a greater chance that tornadoes will develop.

TORNADO SHAPES AND SIZES

Tornadoes come in many different shapes and sizes. Some tornadoes are long and narrow like ropes, with winds of less than 50 miles (80.5 km) per hour. Others can be 1.5 miles (2.5 km) wide, with powerful winds swirling at 300 miles (483 km) per hour. Some tornadoes are shaped like hourglasses; others look like tall columns. Most tornadoes are funnel-shaped—wide at the top and narrow at the bottom.

DID YOU KNOW?

During the months of April, May, and June, anywhere from twenty to forty tornadoes will occur in Tornado Alley each week.

The average tornado funnel is about 800 to 2,000 feet (242 to 606 m) tall. Most funnels are less than 1 mile (1.6 km) wide at the base (the point at which the tip touches the ground). The average width at the base is about 600 to 900 feet (182 to 273 m), but some tips may be only 10 feet (3 m) wide. When a tornado's tip is small, the damage is limited to a narrow path along the ground. The tornado may destroy one house completely, while leaving the house next door to it undamaged.

Outbreaks

Sometimes a cluster of several separate tornadoes hits an area at the same time. This group of tornadoes is known as an outbreak. Outbreaks are far more dangerous and destructive than are single tornadoes.

Multi-vortex Tornadoes

Certain storms will produce a large tornado that has several smaller tornadoes inside its main funnel. This type of tornado is a multi-vortex tornado. A multi-vortex tornado is not

A multi-vortex tornado has several funnels.

the same as an outbreak. A multi-vortex tornado is actually a single storm, with smaller funnels circling around a large center.

Sometimes people refer to multi-vortex tornadoes as killer tornadoes. This is because multi-vortex tornadoes:
- have several funnels
- are much larger and wider than average tornadoes

- have wind speeds of up to 300 miles (483 km) per hour
- can do far more damage than the average tornado

Whirlwinds

Tornadoes are just one type of a natural force known as the whirlwind. Another kind of whirlwind is a waterspout.

Waterspouts are tornadoes that happen over oceans or lakes. A waterspout is a long column of wind that develops in clouds and extends down to the water. Strong winds of up to 200 miles (322 km) per hour suck up the water into the sky. The column can reach as high as 10,000 feet (3,033 km) in the air.

Waterspouts are not very damaging because they don't take place over land. However, they are strong enough to pull sea life from the water and carry it through the air. On July 13, 1949, a waterspout showered a small town in New Zealand with thousands of fish!

A waterspout is a type of tornado that can form over the ocean.

CHAPTER TWO

THE STRONGEST WINDS ON EARTH

The Super Outbreak of April 3 and 4, 1974, was one of the worst natural disasters the United States has ever experienced. The outbreak lasted nearly sixteen hours, with 148 separate tornadoes striking fourteen states.

Alabama was one of the first states to fall victim to the ferocious tornadoes. When a state trooper was asked about the damage done to the small town of Guin, Alabama, he answered, "Guin just isn't there." The rural town was completely destroyed, and nineteen of its citizens were killed.

A few hours later, in Michigan, a group of five young friends was caught in a tornado. They were crossing a bridge in a Volkswagen bus when the tornado struck. The winds picked up the bus and hurtled it off the bridge, 50 feet (14.5 m) down to the water. Only one of the five friends was able to escape and swim

The Super Outbreak of April 3 and 4, 1974, struck fourteen states. It destroyed the town of Xenia, Ohio.

to safety. Her name was Karen Scott. Karen was only seventeen years old when her friends met their watery deaths.

The town that was hit the most directly by the tornadoes was Xenia, Ohio. Five public schools were demolished in Xenia, and thirty-four people were killed. It was very lucky that school had already let out for the day.

When the Super Outbreak finally ended, 315 people were dead and more than 5,400 were injured.

HOW A TORNADO MOVES

The movement of every tornado is different. There are some similarities, however. In the United States, most tornado storms travel diagonally from the southwest to the northeast. On the ground, tornadoes usually move in small, elliptical (oval-shaped) circles. The path of a tornado, if seen from an airplane, looks like someone put a pencil point down on a sheet of

Tornadoes can skip around, destroying some houses while leaving others virtually untouched.

paper and made spirals across the page. A common tornado will loop forward, turn back, cross its own path, loop forward again, and continue in that manner. This random movement is why a tornado can destroy two houses but leave the one between them untouched.

Most tornadoes do not stay in one place for very long. They touch down in one spot for one or two minutes, and then they spin off to another spot. Tornadoes also may skip or hop. Every so often, a tornado will rise up off the ground and then drop back down in a different spot. Tornadoes have been known to skip over houses and leave them undamaged.

How Fast and How Far Can They Move?

Tornadoes move along the ground at an average speed of 20 to 40 miles (32 km to 64 km) per hour. Some tornadoes can move at speeds of up to 60 miles (96.5 km) per hour. They can travel along the ground anywhere from a few hundred feet to more than 100 miles (161 km).

MEASURING TORNADOES

Because tornadoes can be so different in size and strength, a system was created to measure them. In 1971, a professor named T. Theodore

T. Theodore Fujita simulated tornadoes to create the F-scale.

Fujita came up with the Fujita scale, or F-scale. The scale is based mainly on the wind speeds inside a tornado and the damage these winds can do.

The F-scale classifies a tornado on a scale from 0 to 5 (or F-0 to F-5). An F-0 tornado is rather harmless. An F-5, on the other hand, is the kind of killer tornado that destroys towns and cities.

TORNADOES

Tornadoes of F-0 and F-1 strength mostly damage windows and rip loose objects from buildings. An F-2 tornado can tear roofs off houses, destroy mobile homes, and uproot large trees. An F-3 tornado can destroy the walls of a house and can overturn train cars. A direct hit from an F-4 tornado leaves a house looking like a pile of rubble. An F-4 tornado also is strong enough to lift cars and toss them through the air. In the rare case of an F-5 tornado, a house can be lifted off its foundation and carried several miles before it is smashed to the ground. An F-5 tornado can even destroy concrete and steel structures.

Using the Fujita scale, scientists have determined that about 70 percent of tornadoes are of F-0 or F-1 intensity. These are called weak tornadoes. Weak tornadoes last anywhere from sixty seconds to just under twenty minutes. Less than 5 percent of tornado deaths are caused by weak tornadoes.

An F-4 tornado is capable of lifting cars into the air and tossing them to the ground.

Strong tornadoes (F-2 and F-3) account for 29 percent of all tornadoes. These storms may last anywhere from twenty minutes to just under an hour. Strong tornadoes are responsible for 30 percent of tornado-related deaths.

Only 2 percent of all tornadoes are violent tornadoes (F-4 or F-5). These powerful storms can last for an hour or more. Although violent tornadoes rarely occur, they are responsible for 70 percent of all tornado deaths.

MEASURING TORNADO POWER

The Fujita scale is the best method scientists have to classify tornadoes. However, there are other factors to look at when determining a tornado's strength or intensity. First, it is the wind speed, and not the actual size of the tornado, that determines the damage it can do. A large tornado can be weak, while small tornadoes can be extremely violent. Second, if a tornado capable of F-4 damage strikes an unpopulated area, it may produce only F-2 damage. Similarly, if an F-1 tornado—with wind speeds of about 70 miles (113 km) per hour—strikes a busy city, it can produce the kind of damage done by an F-3 tornado.

Even a small tornado, such as this one that occurred on July 20, 1999, near the Kennedy Space Center, can cause serious damage.

CHAPTER THREE

STUDYING TORNADOES

In one of the deadliest storms in years, an outbreak of tornadoes ripped through Oklahoma and Kansas on May 3 and 4 of 1999. Oklahoma suffered the most damage—more than seventy tornadoes touched down in the state. Some tornadoes were more than 1 mile (1.6 km) wide with wind speeds of more than 200 miles (322 km) per hour. Fifty-two twisters hit the state's capitol, Oklahoma City.

Scientists from the University of Oklahoma chased the twisters in a truck equipped with Doppler radar. Doppler radar can record the wind speeds inside a tornado. One tornado that the scientists observed—an F-5 tornado that hit the capitol—had the fastest wind speeds ever known on Earth. Winds inside this tornado were clocked at 318 miles (512 km) an hour.

This mother and child survived the deadly tornado outbreak of May 3 and 4, 1999.

TORNADO PREDICTION

Scientists who study the weather and the atmosphere are called meteorologists. They study weather patterns to try to figure out when tornadoes may occur. Tornadoes are hard to predict, but there are methods that meteorologists can use to make accurate predictions.

Observing Thunderstorm Clouds

Meteorologists pay attention to the size and shape of developing thunderstorms. The storms that are strong enough to produce tornadoes—tornadic thunderstorms—usually have a specific shape. A tornadic thunderstorm is anvil-shaped—the bottom and the top of the storm are flat, and its middle is thin. If a bubble is sticking out of the flat top of a storm cloud, it means there is a lot of high air pressure and violent wind activity inside the storm. When a storm has this shape and size, a tornado may be forming.

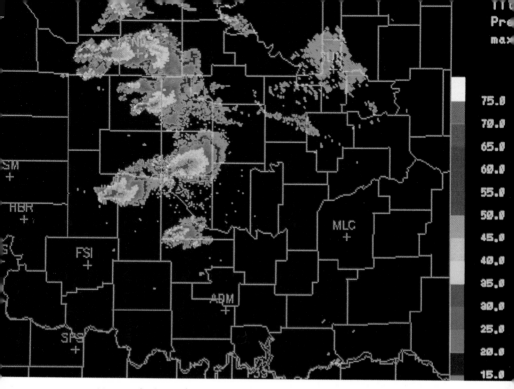

75.0
70.0
65.0
60.0
55.0
50.0
45.0
40.0
35.0
30.0
25.0
20.0
15.0

Meteorologists use Doppler radar to detect major storms that may produce tornadoes.

Doppler Radar

The most effective tool in trying to forecast tornadoes is Doppler radar. Doppler radar has been used to detect major storms and tornadoes since 1971. Doppler radar records the location and strength of storm systems. It tracks wind speed, records shifts in wind activity, and measures rain, snow, and hail carried by winds. Shifting winds are thought to be the first sign that a tornado may form.

The Optical Transient Detector

The most recent advance in predicting tornadoes is the study of lightning. In 1995, the National Air and Space Association (NASA) started recording how often lightning occurred in thunderstorms. Lightning was measured by a low-flying satellite called the Optical Transient Detector (OTD). Using the OTD, scientists were able to record the number of lightning flashes in a certain area. Meteorologists now know that tornadoes are produced by the same conditions that produce large amounts of lightning in a storm. They observe the amount of lightning in a storm to help them predict tornadoes.

Storm Chasers

In the spring of 1994 and 1995, scientists carried out a daring project called VORTEX. Using cars equipped with radar systems, the scientists drove near, in, and around severe

Scientists who participated in the VORTEX project used vans specially equipped with radar systems.

thunderstorms. They recorded the temperature, humidity, and wind speed in the storms. They used the radar to observe the shifting winds inside the storms. In addition, two planes with their own radar systems scanned the tops of the storms.

The information gathered from these storms was used to create a computer model of a tornado. VORTEX data has helped scientists to better understand the weather conditions present when a tornado forms.

TORNADO WATCHES AND WARNINGS

The chance that you will experience a tornado is slim. Even in areas with heavy tornado activity, a tornado isn't likely to strike any one place more than once in every 250 years. However, because these storms can be deadly, it's important to know when a tornado may occur in your area. The first thing to know is the difference between a tornado warning and a tornado watch. A tornado watch means that a tornado is possible in your area. A tornado warning is issued when a tornado has actually been spotted and is headed toward the area.

The National Weather Service will issue and update tornado watches and warnings on television and radio. Stay tuned and be alert to any changes in the weather. Strong winds, hail, fast-moving clouds, debris dropping from the sky, or the sound of roaring wind can signal that a tornado is on its way.

Severe weather such as strong winds and dark, fast-moving clouds, can signal that a tornado is on its way.

Fact Sheet ·········

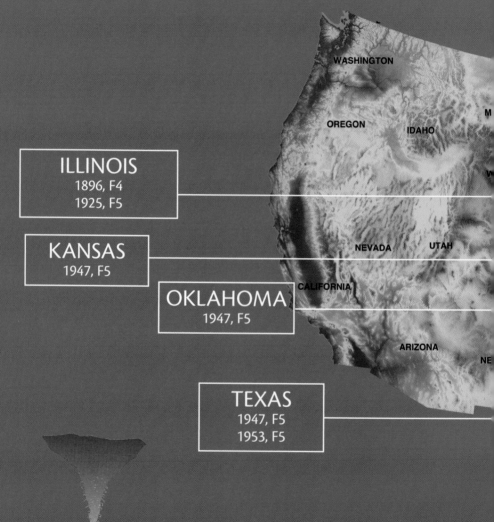

WASHINGTON

OREGON   IDAHO   M

ILLINOIS
1896, F4
1925, F5

KANSAS
1947, F5   NEVADA   UTAH

OKLAHOMA   CALIFORNIA
1947, F5

                                        ARIZONA
                                                    NE

TEXAS
1947, F5
1953, F5

The tornado symbol marks where the
deadliest tornadoes occurred.

Deadliest U.S. Tornadoes

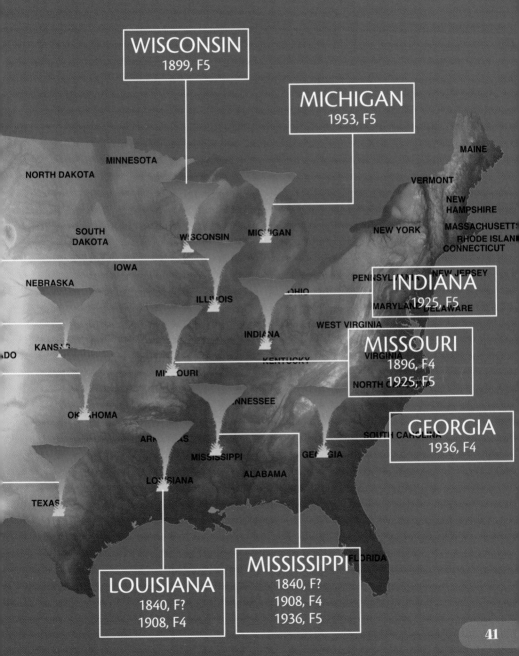

WISCONSIN
1899, F5

MICHIGAN
1953, F5

INDIANA
1925, F5

MISSOURI
1896, F4
1925, F5

GEORGIA
1936, F4

LOUISIANA
1840, F?
1908, F4

MISSISSIPPI
1840, F?
1908, F4
1936, F5

MAINE

VERMONT

NEW HAMPSHIRE

MASSACHUSETTS
RHODE ISLAND
CONNECTICUT

NEW YORK

NEW JERSEY

PENNSYLVANIA

MARYLAND
DELAWARE

WEST VIRGINIA

VIRGINIA

NORTH CAROLINA

SOUTH CAROLINA

MINNESOTA

NORTH DAKOTA

SOUTH DAKOTA

WISCONSIN

MICHIGAN

IOWA

NEBRASKA

ILLINOIS

OHIO

INDIANA

KANSAS

KENTUCKY

COLORADO

MISSOURI

TENNESSEE

OKLAHOMA

ARKANSAS

MISSISSIPPI

GEORGIA

ALABAMA

LOUISIANA

TEXAS

FLORIDA

NEW WORDS

air pressure the weight of an air mass in the atmosphere pressing down on any one spot

atmosphere the thin layer of air surrounding Earth

condense to change from a gas into a liquid

condensation the process in which water vapor turns into a liquid

Doppler radar radar that detects and measures precipitation and wind activity

elliptical oval-shaped

F-scale the measurement scale that classifies tornadoes according to their wind speeds

funnel rapidly spinning winds that form the center of a tornado

hail small pieces of ice

humidity moisture or dampness

jet stream a weather pattern of strong winds and low air pressure

meteorologists scientists who study weather

multi-vortex tornado a tornado that has two or more small funnels that spin around a main funnel

NEW WORDS

National Weather Service a government agency responsible for observing and forecasting weather

Optical Transient Detector (OTD) a low-flying satellite that detects lightning flashes in storms

outbreak a storm that produces several tornadoes in the same area at the same time

tornadic thunderstorm a severe thunderstorm capable of producing a tornado

tornado a rapidly spinning column of air that comes into contact with the ground

Tornado Alley an area of millions of square miles in the middle of the United States where tornadoes are very common

tornado warning an announcement that a tornado is possible in an area

tornado watch an announcement that a tornado has been spotted in an area

updraft strong vertical winds that flow up from the ground into clouds

NEW WORDS

vacuum something that sucks up whatever is near it

waterspout a tornado that happens over a body of water

water vapor water in the form of a gas

whirlwind any storm with strong, swirling winds, such as a tornado

Allaby, Michael. *Tornadoes*. New York: Facts on File, 1997.

Ehrlbach, Arlene. *Tornadoes*. Danbury, CT: Children's Press, 1994.

Galiano, Dean. *Tornadoes, The Weather Watcher's Library.* New York: Rosen Publishing Group, 2000.

Herman, Gail. *Storm Chasers: Tracking Twisters.* New York: Putnam, 1997.

Lampton, Christopher. *Tornado, A Disaster Book.* Brookfield, CT: Millbrook Press, 1998.

Rose, Sally. *Tornadoes*. New York: Simon and Schuster's Children, 1999.

Simon, Seymour. *Tornadoes*. New York: Morrow Junior, 1999.

RESOURCES

FEMA Fact Sheet: Tornadoes
www.fema.gov/library/tornadof.htm
This site gives advanced planning and quick response tips for surviving a tornado, from the Federal Emergency Management Agency (FEMA). It includes a list of supplies to keep on hand in case of an emergency, and instructions for how to proceed after a tornado.

Tornado Project
P.O. Box 302
St. Johnsbury, VT 05819
Web site: *www.tornadoproject.com*
The Tornado Project gathers information about tornadoes and prints books, posters, and videos in an effort to educate the public about tornadoes.

INDEX

INDEX

ABOUT THE AUTHOR

Luke Thompson was born in Delaware. He holds a degree in English literature from James Madison University. He lives in Vail, Colorado.